JAN 15

JR. GRAPHIC GHOST STORIES

# THE FLYING DUTCHMAN

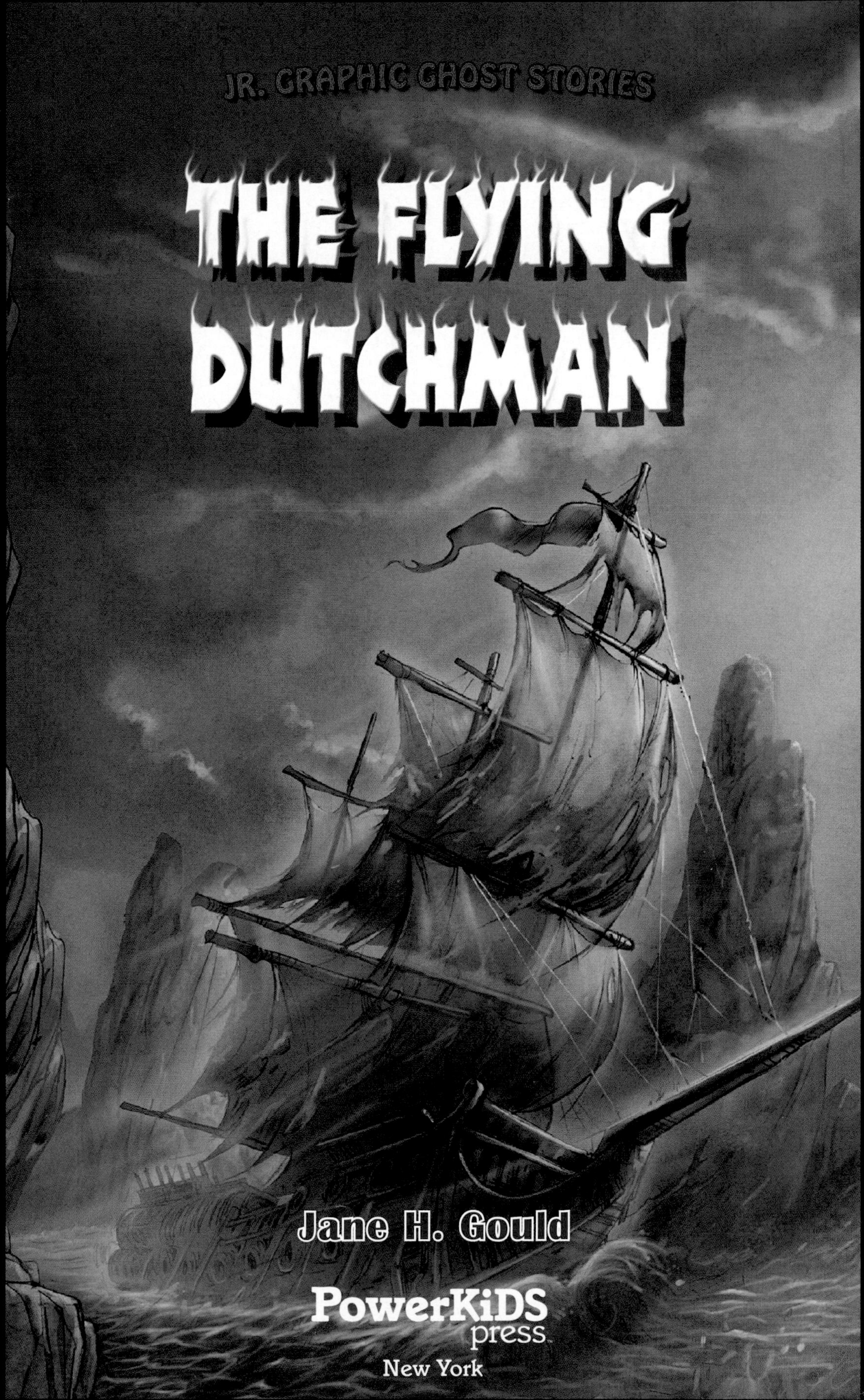

Jane H. Gould

PowerKiDS press.
New York

Published in 2015 by The Rosen Publishing Group, Inc.
29 East 21st Street, New York, NY 10010

First Edition

Editor: Joanne Randolph
Book Design: Contentra Technologies
Illustrations: Contentra Technologies

**Publisher's Cataloging Data**

Gould, Jane H.
The Flying Dutchman / by Jane H. Gould — first edition.
p. cm. — (Jr. graphic ghost stories)
Includes index.
ISBN 978-1-4777-7088-7 (library binding) — ISBN 978-1-4777-7089-4 (pbk.) —
ISBN 978-1-4777-7090-0 (6-pack)
1. Folklore — Netherlands — Juvenile literature. 2. Folklore — Juvenile literature.
I. Gould, Jane H. II. Title.
PZ8.1 G68 2015
398—d23

Manufactured in the United States of America

CPSIA Compliance Information: Batch #WS14PK2: For Further Information contact Rosen
Publishing, New York, New York at 1-800-237-9932

# Contents



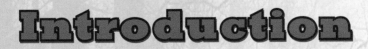

# Introduction

Imagine being a sailor on a ship in the ocean. Suddenly, the skies turn dark, lightning crackles, and the waves swell. What could have caused this unexpected storm? You look into the clouds and see what looks like an old-fashioned sailing ship and its ghostly crew. Could it be the *Flying Dutchman*?

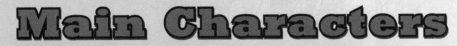

# Main Characters

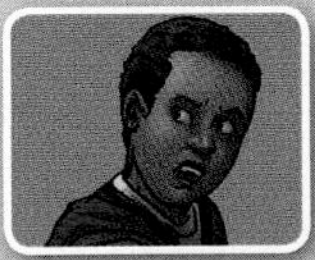

**Jack** An 11-year-old boy.

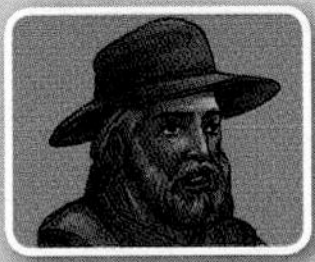

**Grandpa** Jack's grandfather.

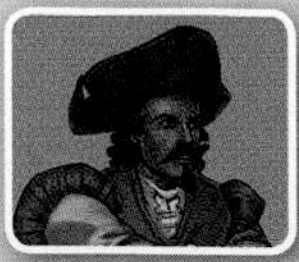

**Hendrick Vanderdecken** (ca. 1600s) The captain of the *Flying Dutchman.*

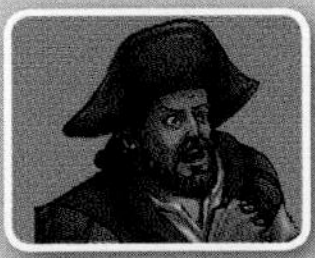

**Mr. Thompson** (ca. 1600s) Captain Vanderdecken's **first mate** on the *Flying Dutchman.*

# The Flying Dutchman

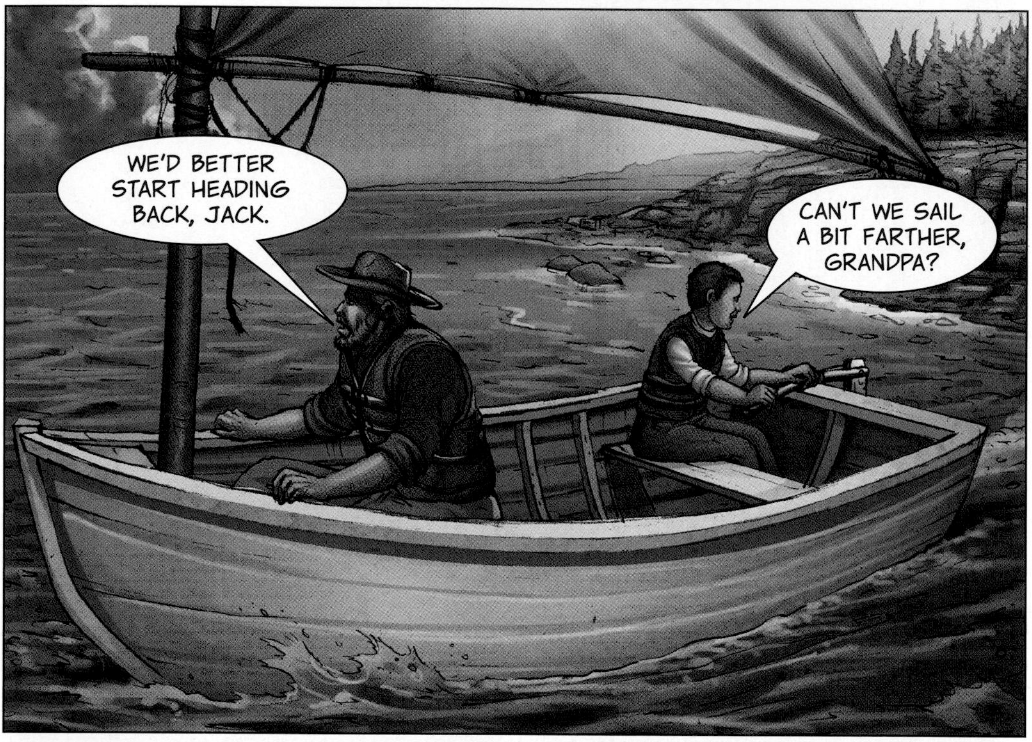
WE'D BETTER START HEADING BACK, JACK.
CAN'T WE SAIL A BIT FARTHER, GRANDPA?

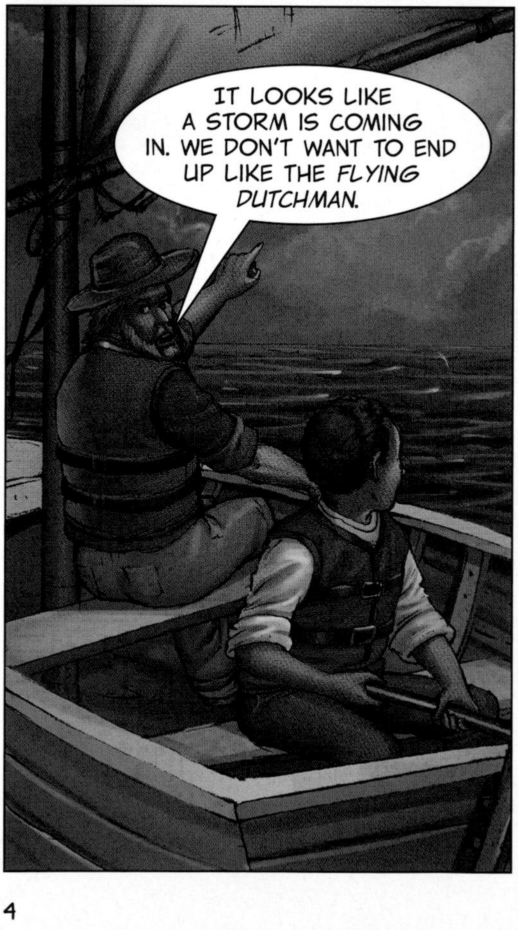
IT LOOKS LIKE A STORM IS COMING IN. WE DON'T WANT TO END UP LIKE THE *FLYING DUTCHMAN*.

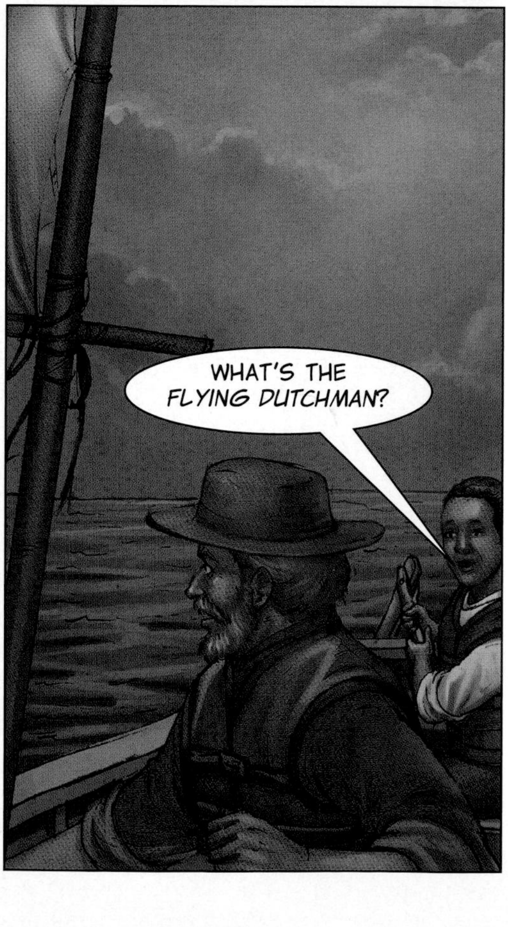
WHAT'S THE *FLYING DUTCHMAN*?

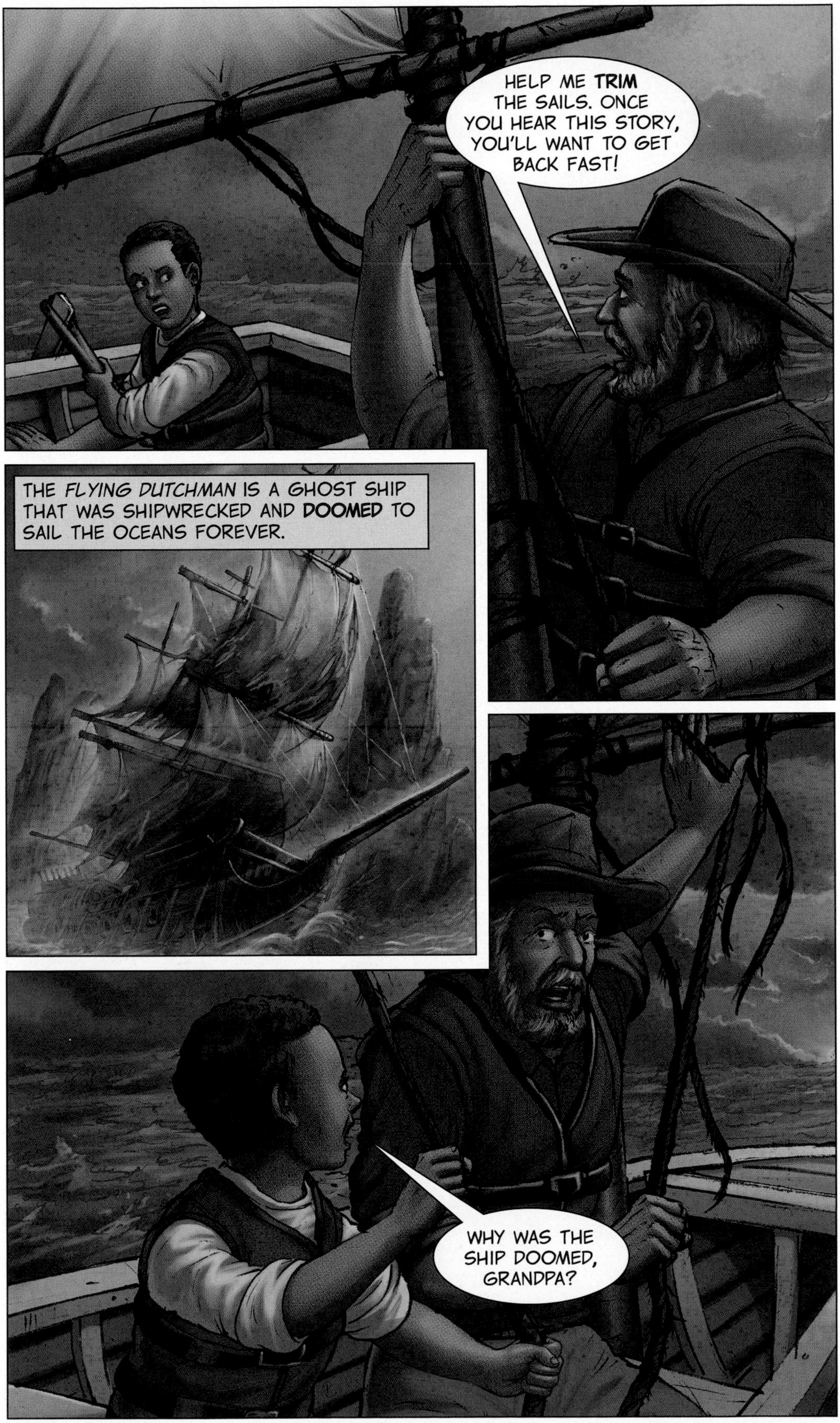
HELP ME TRIM THE SAILS. ONCE YOU HEAR THIS STORY, YOU'LL WANT TO GET BACK FAST!
THE FLYING DUTCHMAN IS A GHOST SHIP THAT WAS SHIPWRECKED AND DOOMED TO SAIL THE OCEANS FOREVER.
WHY WAS THE SHIP DOOMED, GRANDPA?

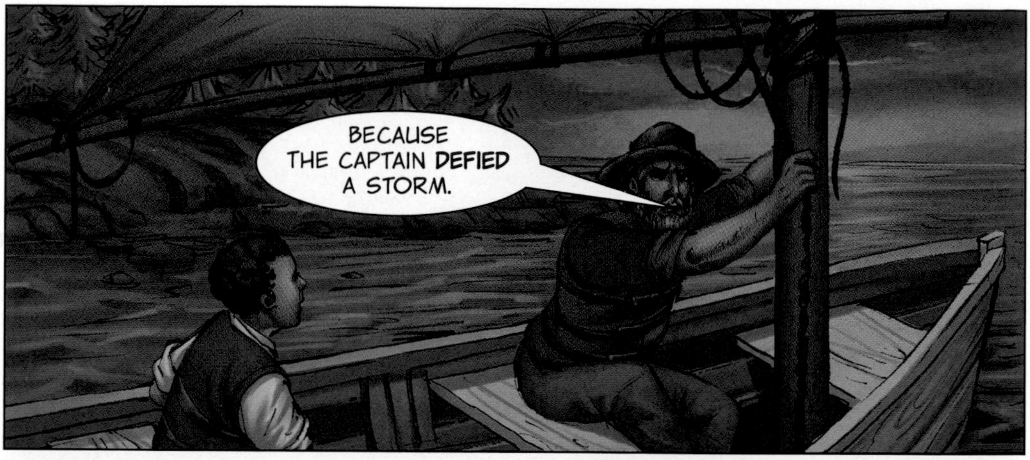
BECAUSE THE CAPTAIN **DEFIED** A STORM.

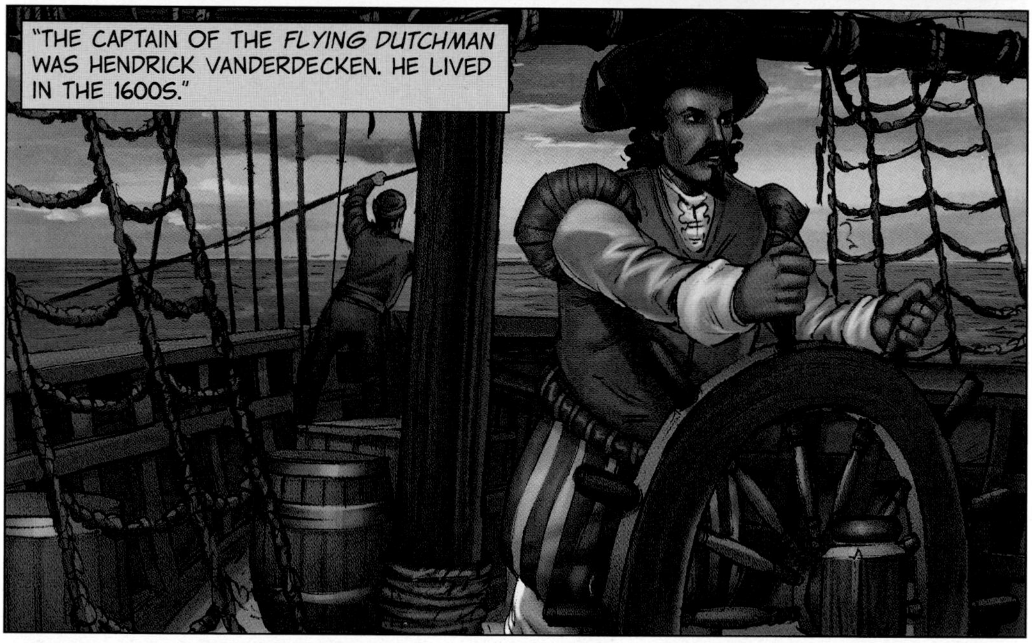
"THE CAPTAIN OF THE *FLYING DUTCHMAN* WAS HENDRICK VANDERDECKEN. HE LIVED IN THE 1600S."

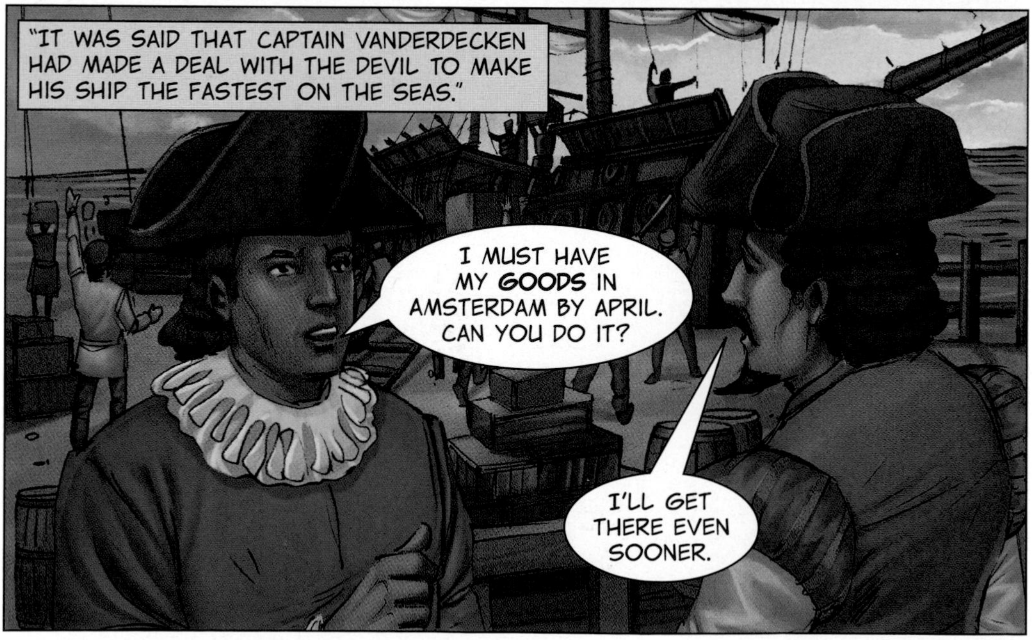
"IT WAS SAID THAT CAPTAIN VANDERDECKEN HAD MADE A DEAL WITH THE DEVIL TO MAKE HIS SHIP THE FASTEST ON THE SEAS."
I MUST HAVE MY **GOODS** IN AMSTERDAM BY APRIL. CAN YOU DO IT?
I'LL GET THERE EVEN SOONER.

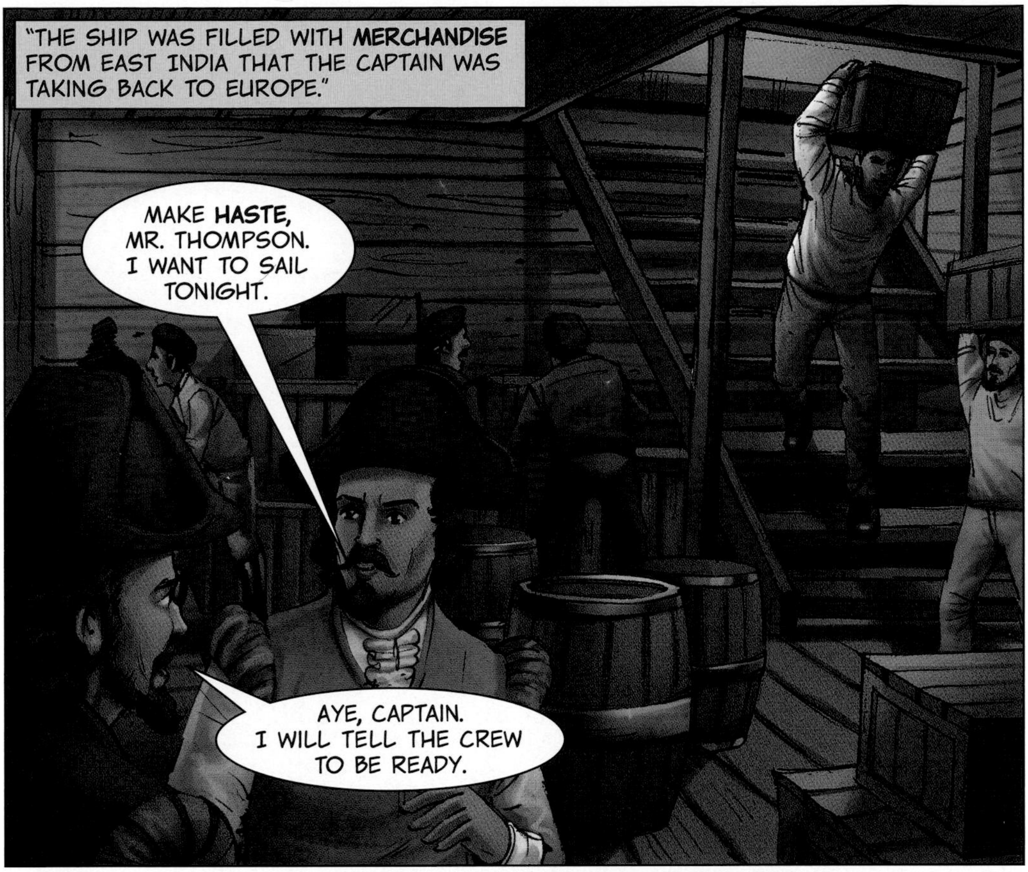
"THE SHIP WAS FILLED WITH MERCHANDISE FROM EAST INDIA THAT THE CAPTAIN WAS TAKING BACK TO EUROPE."
MAKE HASTE, MR. THOMPSON. I WANT TO SAIL TONIGHT.
AYE, CAPTAIN. I WILL TELL THE CREW TO BE READY.

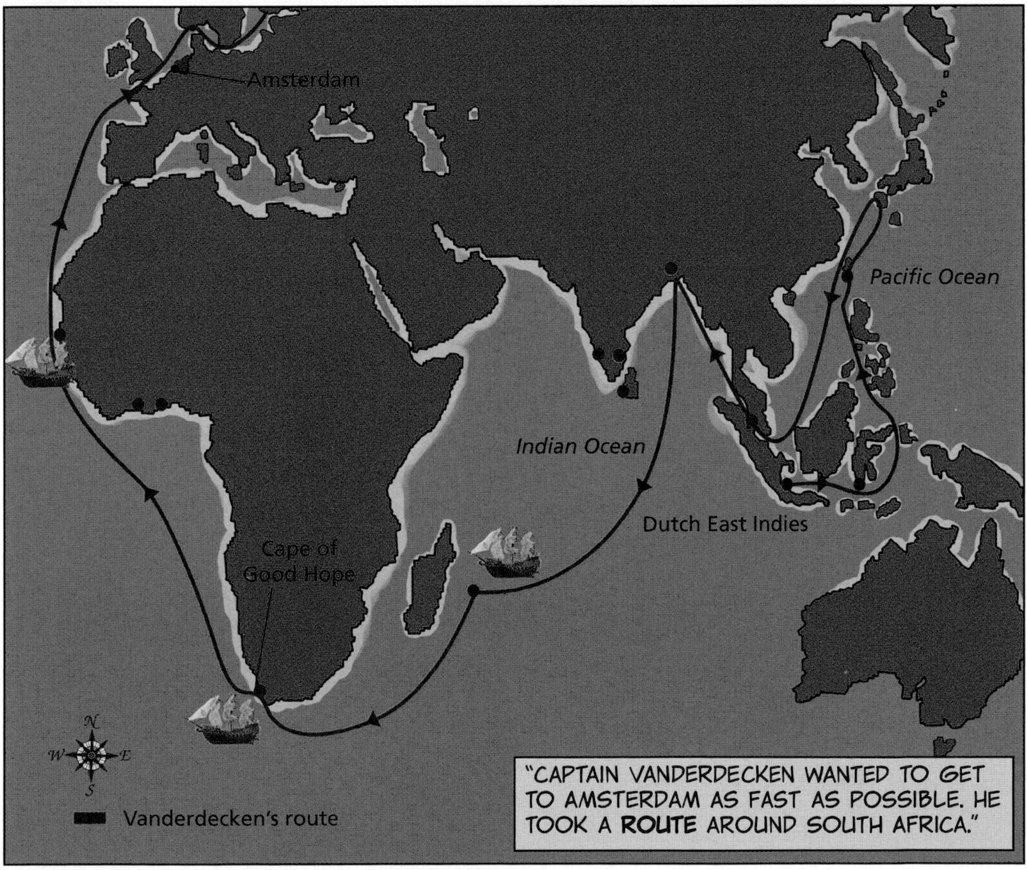
Amsterdam
Pacific Ocean
Indian Ocean
Dutch East Indies
Cape of Good Hope
N
W
E
S
Vanderdecken's route
"CAPTAIN VANDERDECKEN WANTED TO GET TO AMSTERDAM AS FAST AS POSSIBLE. HE TOOK A ROUTE AROUND SOUTH AFRICA."

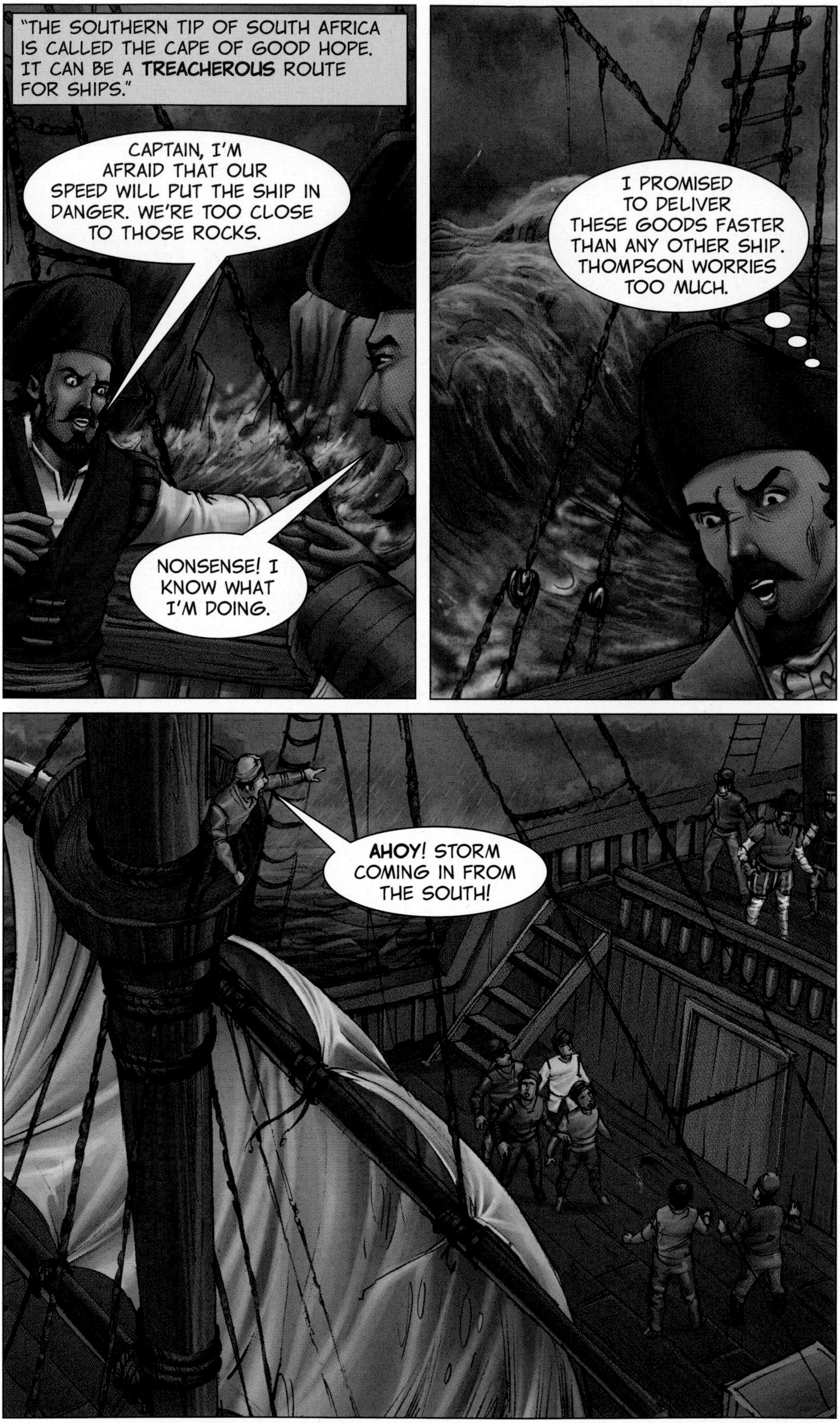
"THE SOUTHERN TIP OF SOUTH AFRICA IS CALLED THE CAPE OF GOOD HOPE. IT CAN BE A **TREACHEROUS** ROUTE FOR SHIPS."
CAPTAIN, I'M AFRAID THAT OUR SPEED WILL PUT THE SHIP IN DANGER. WE'RE TOO CLOSE TO THOSE ROCKS.
NONSENSE! I KNOW WHAT I'M DOING.
I PROMISED TO DELIVER THESE GOODS FASTER THAN ANY OTHER SHIP. THOMPSON WORRIES TOO MUCH.
**AHOY**! STORM COMING IN FROM THE SOUTH!

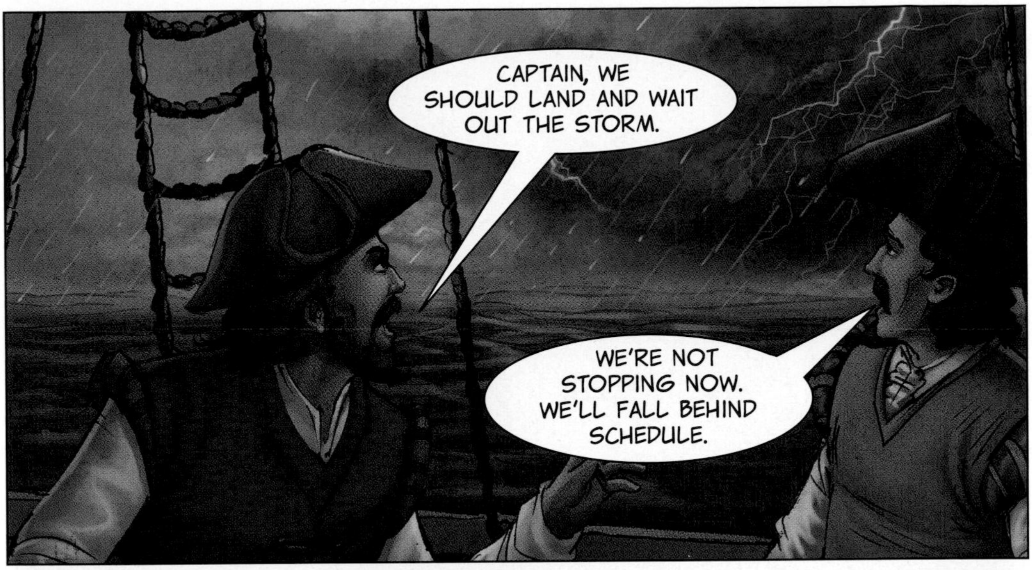
CAPTAIN, WE SHOULD LAND AND WAIT OUT THE STORM.
WE'RE NOT STOPPING NOW. WE'LL FALL BEHIND SCHEDULE.

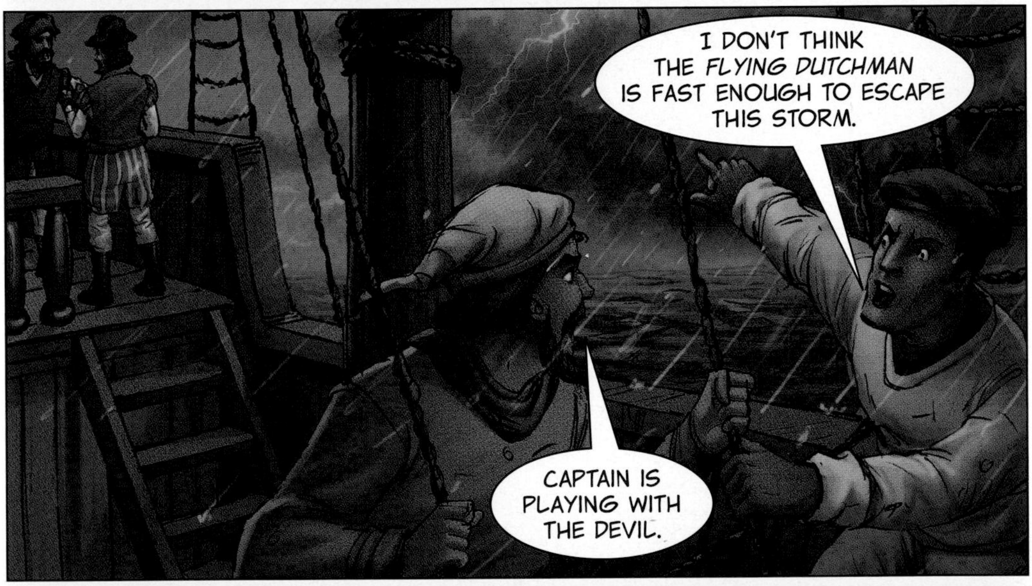
I DON'T THINK THE *FLYING DUTCHMAN* IS FAST ENOUGH TO ESCAPE THIS STORM.
CAPTAIN IS PLAYING WITH THE DEVIL.

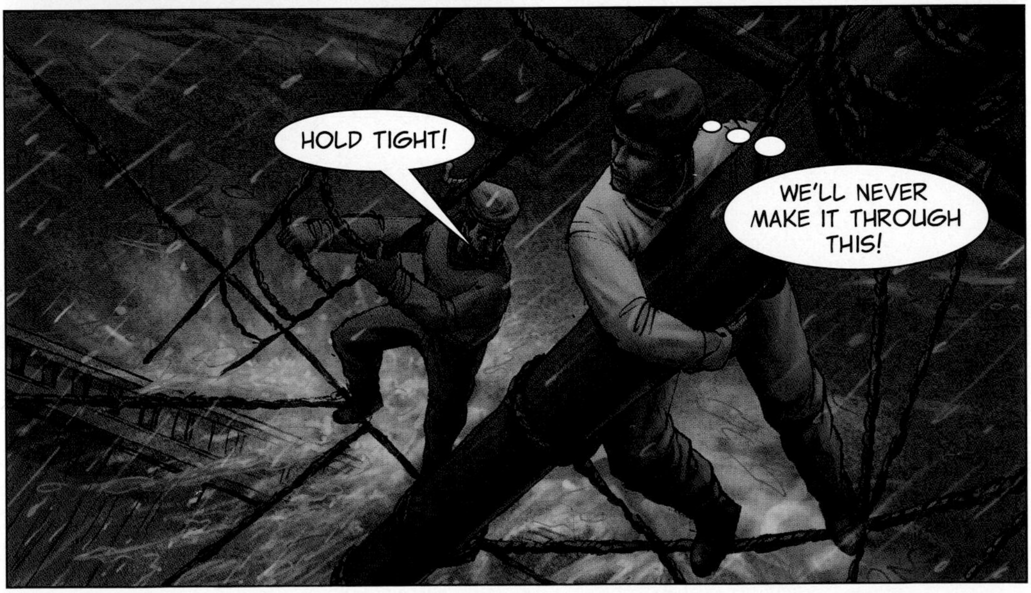
HOLD TIGHT!
WE'LL NEVER MAKE IT THROUGH THIS!

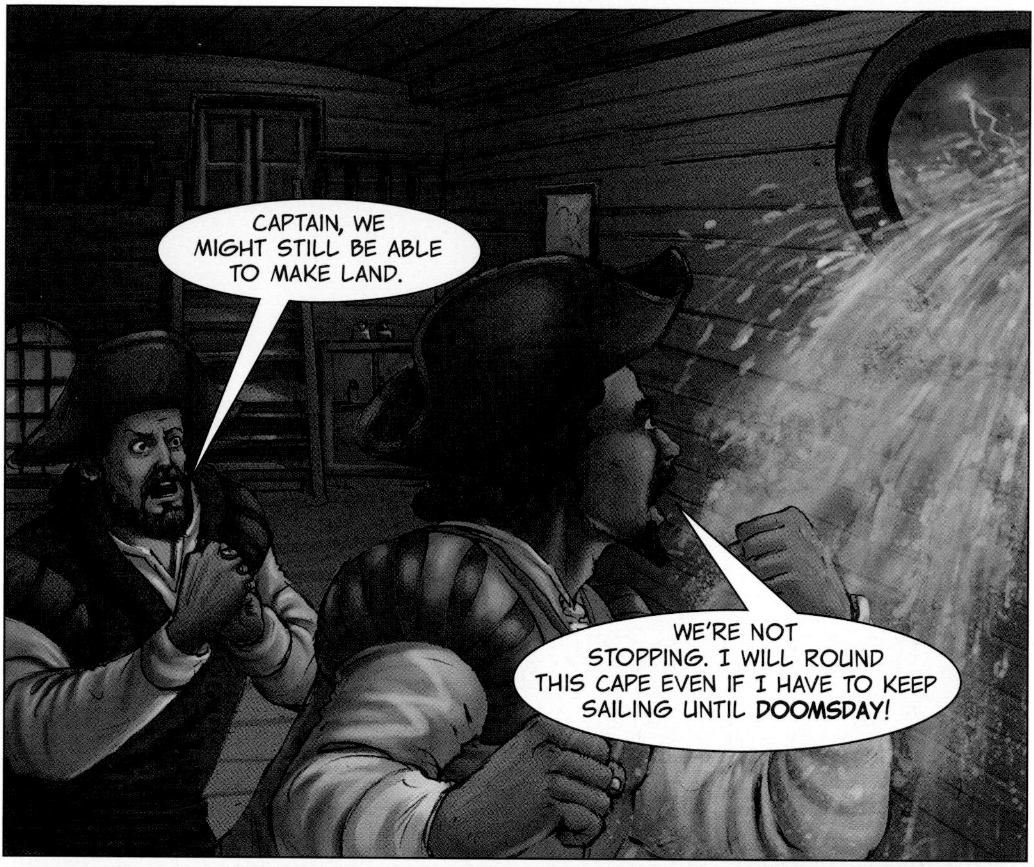
CAPTAIN, WE MIGHT STILL BE ABLE TO MAKE LAND.
WE'RE NOT STOPPING. I WILL ROUND THIS CAPE EVEN IF I HAVE TO KEEP SAILING UNTIL **DOOMSDAY**!

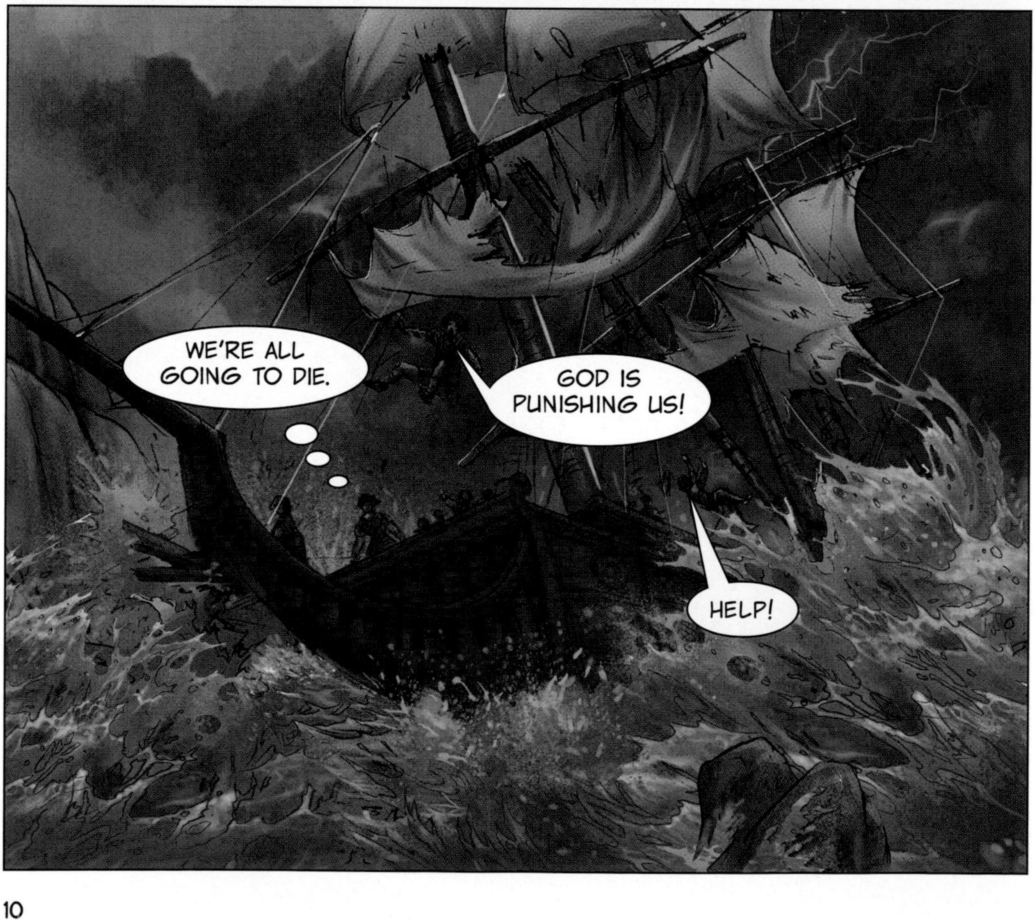
WE'RE ALL GOING TO DIE.
GOD IS PUNISHING US!
HELP!

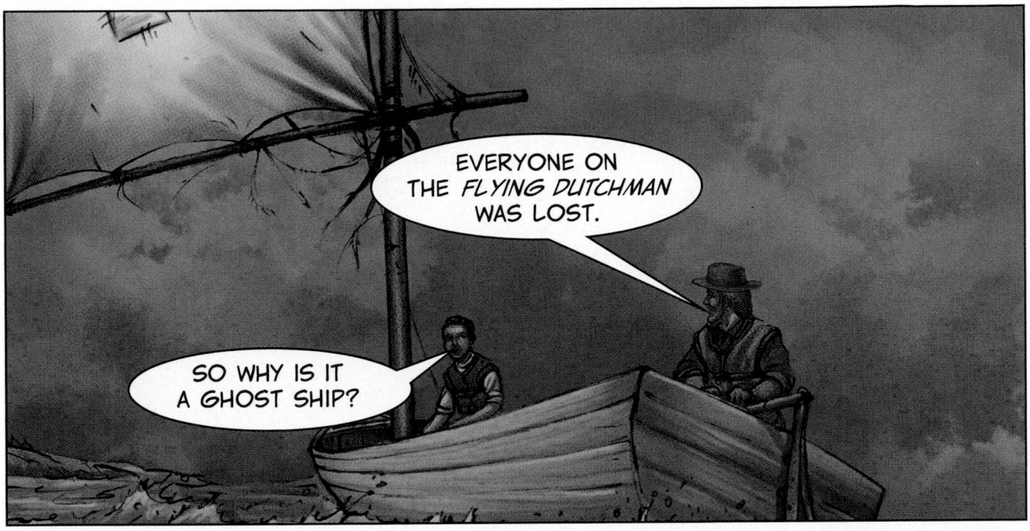
SO WHY IS IT A GHOST SHIP?
EVERYONE ON THE *FLYING DUTCHMAN* WAS LOST.

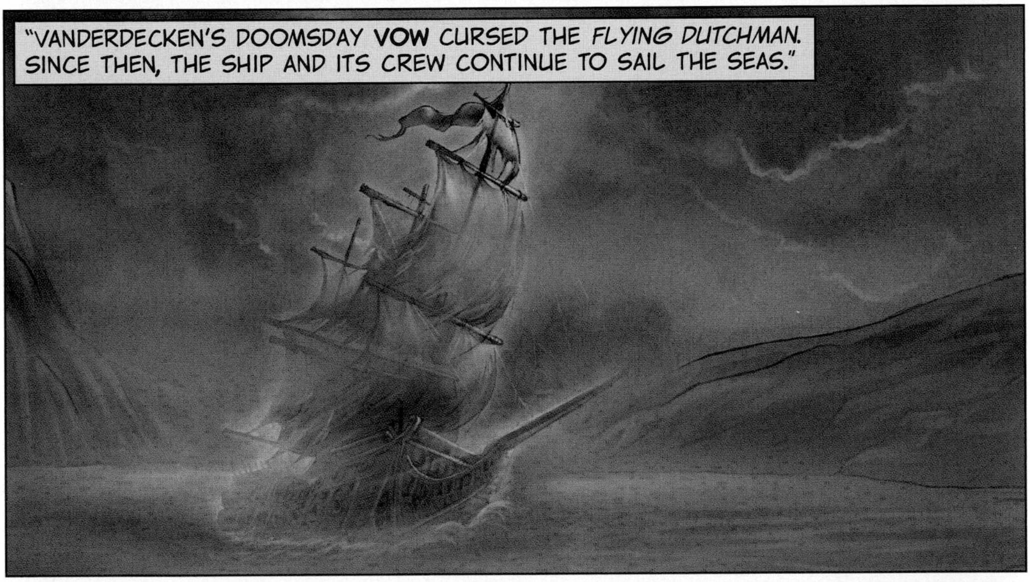
"VANDERDECKEN'S DOOMSDAY **VOW** CURSED THE *FLYING DUTCHMAN*. SINCE THEN, THE SHIP AND ITS CREW CONTINUE TO SAIL THE SEAS."

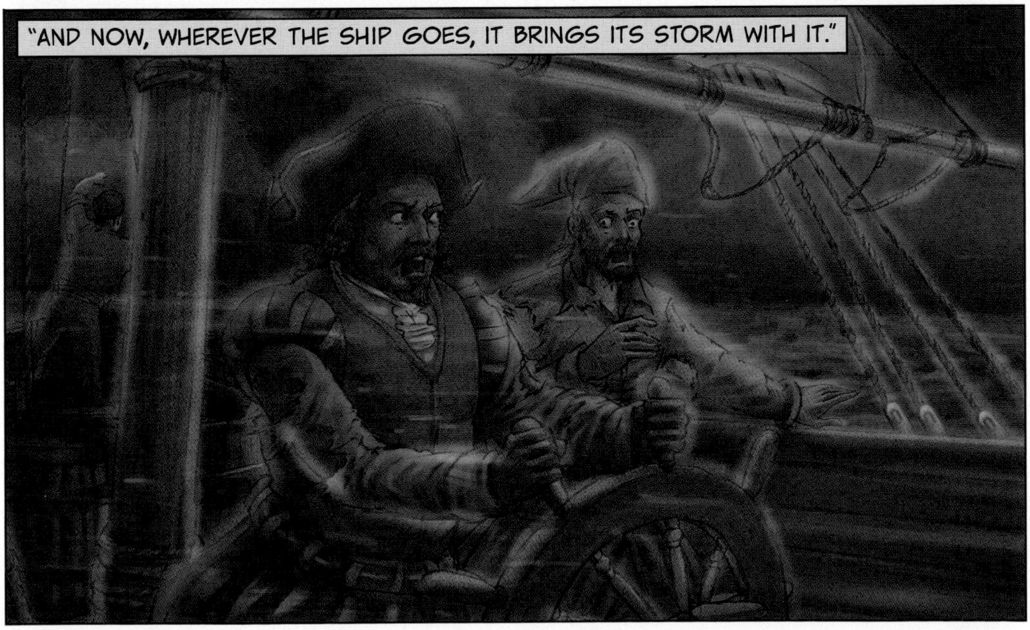
"AND NOW, WHEREVER THE SHIP GOES, IT BRINGS ITS STORM WITH IT."

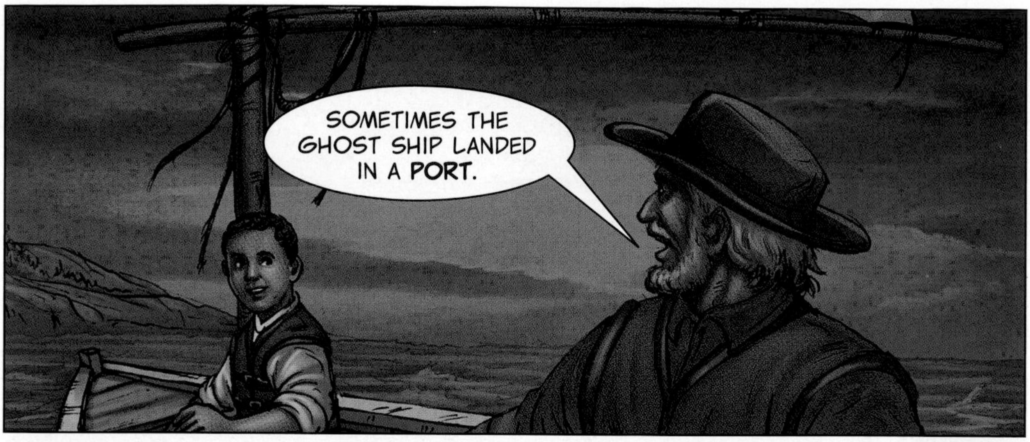
SOMETIMES THE GHOST SHIP LANDED IN A PORT.

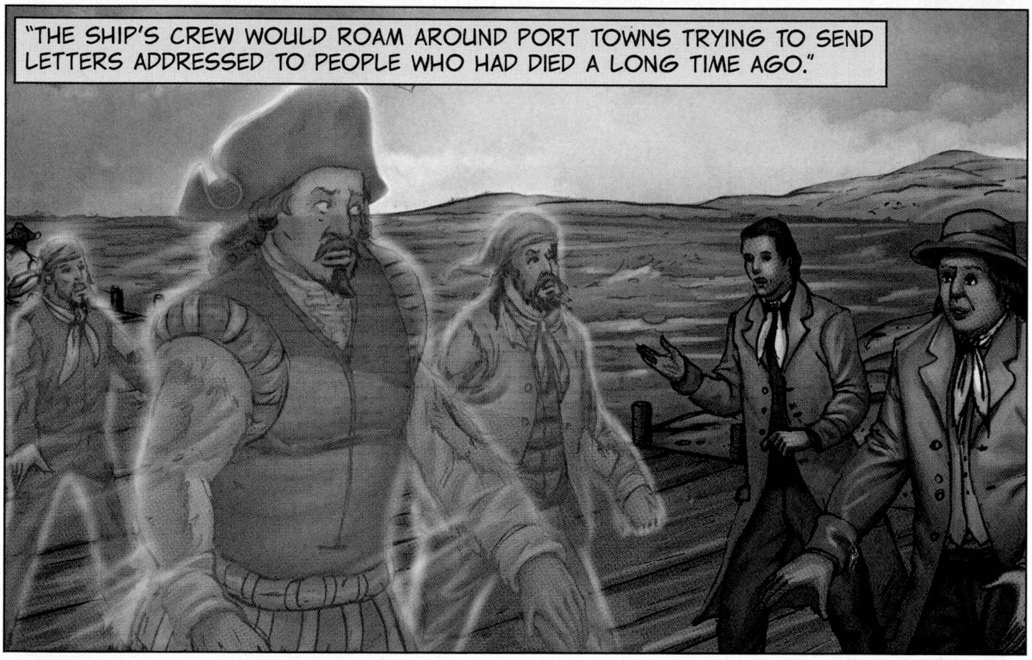
"THE SHIP'S CREW WOULD ROAM AROUND PORT TOWNS TRYING TO SEND LETTERS ADDRESSED TO PEOPLE WHO HAD DIED A LONG TIME AGO."

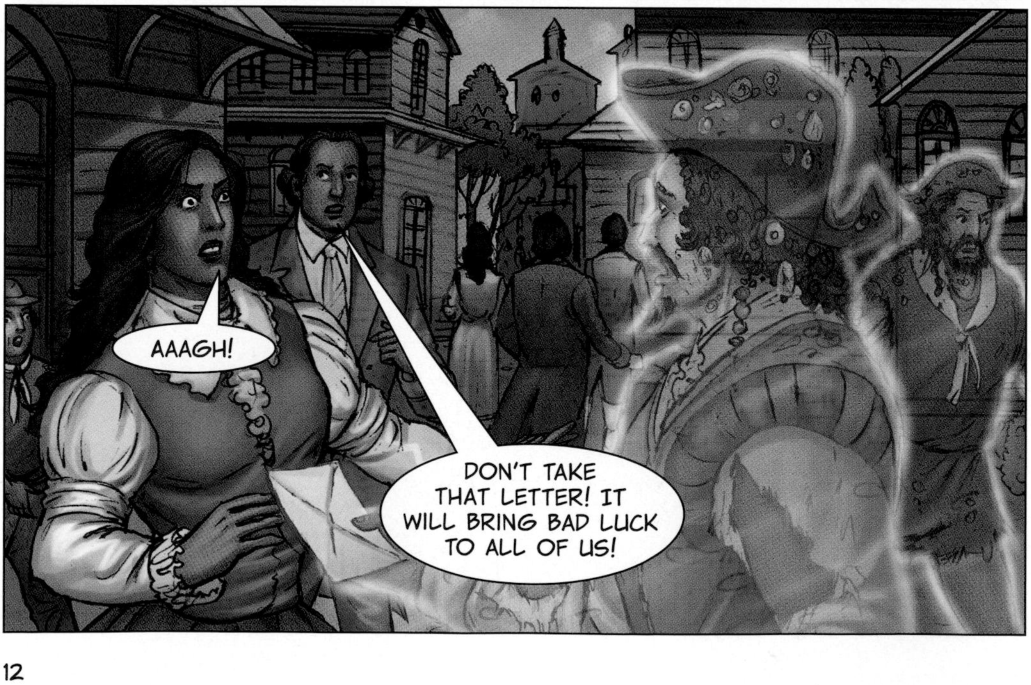
AAAGH!
DON'T TAKE THAT LETTER! IT WILL BRING BAD LUCK TO ALL OF US!

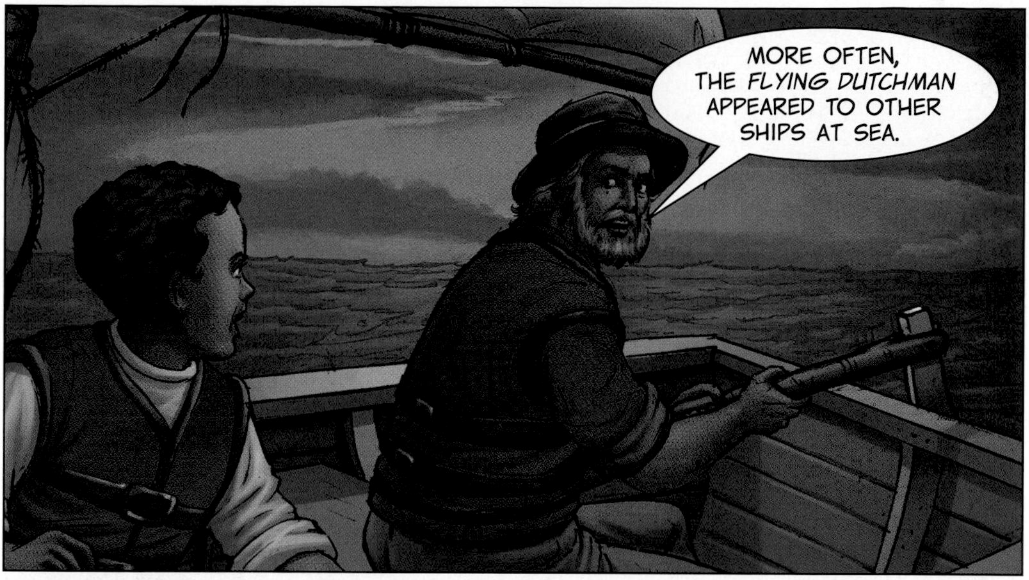
MORE OFTEN, THE FLYING DUTCHMAN APPEARED TO OTHER SHIPS AT SEA.

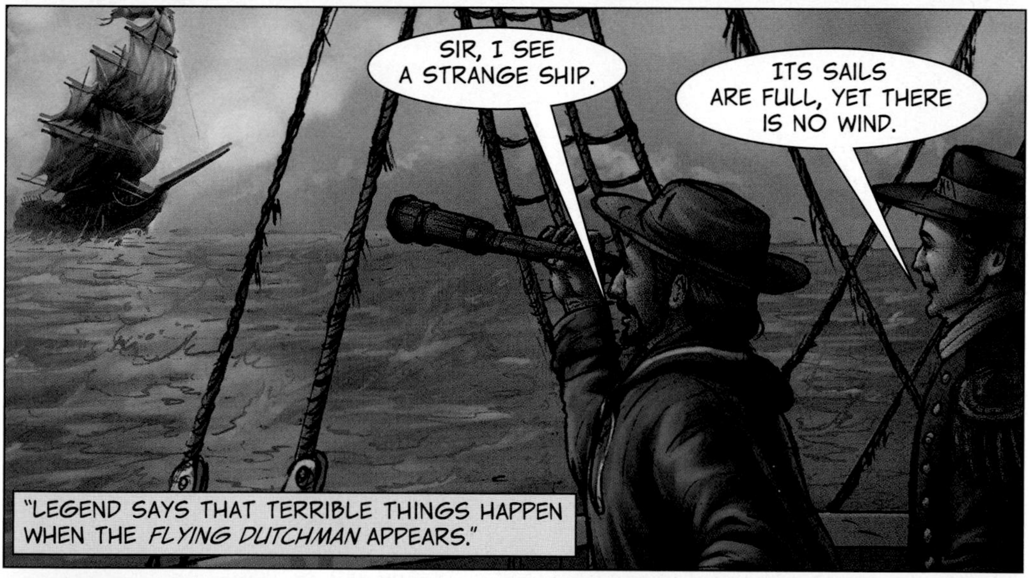
SIR, I SEE A STRANGE SHIP.
ITS SAILS ARE FULL, YET THERE IS NO WIND.
"LEGEND SAYS THAT TERRIBLE THINGS HAPPEN WHEN THE FLYING DUTCHMAN APPEARS."

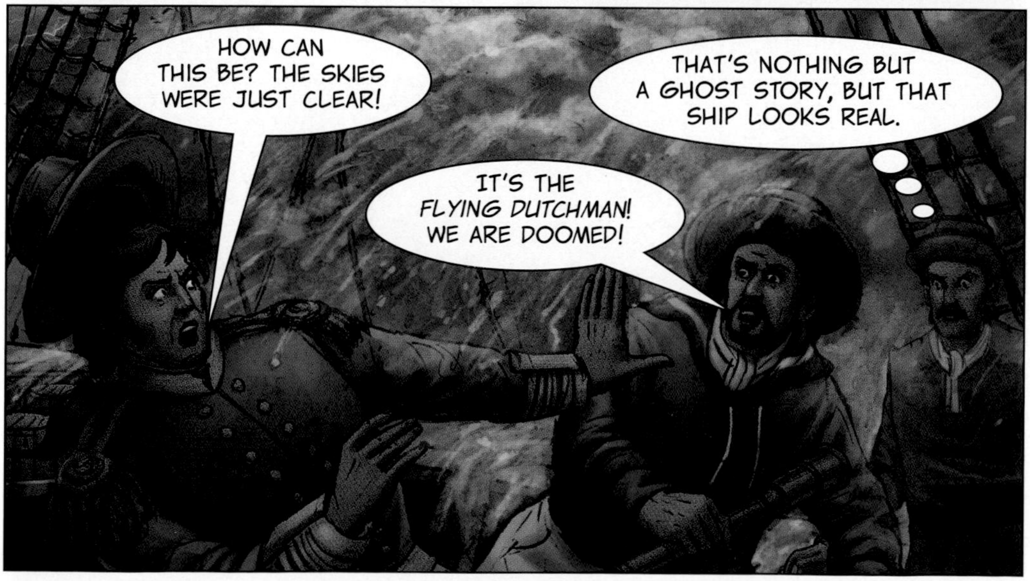
HOW CAN THIS BE? THE SKIES WERE JUST CLEAR!
THAT'S NOTHING BUT A GHOST STORY, BUT THAT SHIP LOOKS REAL.
IT'S THE FLYING DUTCHMAN! WE ARE DOOMED!

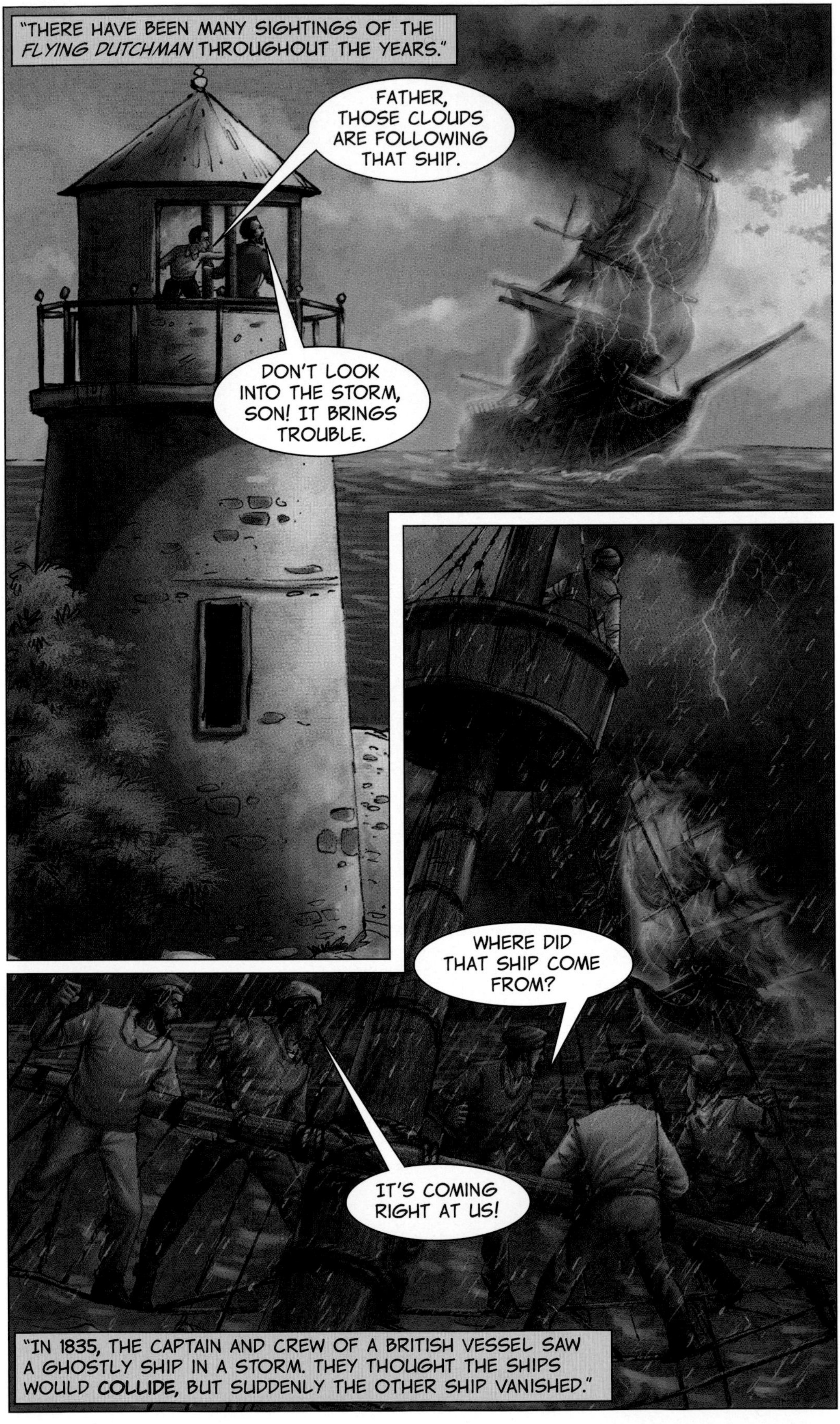
"THERE HAVE BEEN MANY SIGHTINGS OF THE *FLYING DUTCHMAN* THROUGHOUT THE YEARS."
FATHER, THOSE CLOUDS ARE FOLLOWING THAT SHIP.
DON'T LOOK INTO THE STORM, SON! IT BRINGS TROUBLE.
WHERE DID THAT SHIP COME FROM?
IT'S COMING RIGHT AT US!
"IN 1835, THE CAPTAIN AND CREW OF A BRITISH VESSEL SAW A GHOSTLY SHIP IN A STORM. THEY THOUGHT THE SHIPS WOULD **COLLIDE**, BUT SUDDENLY THE OTHER SHIP VANISHED."

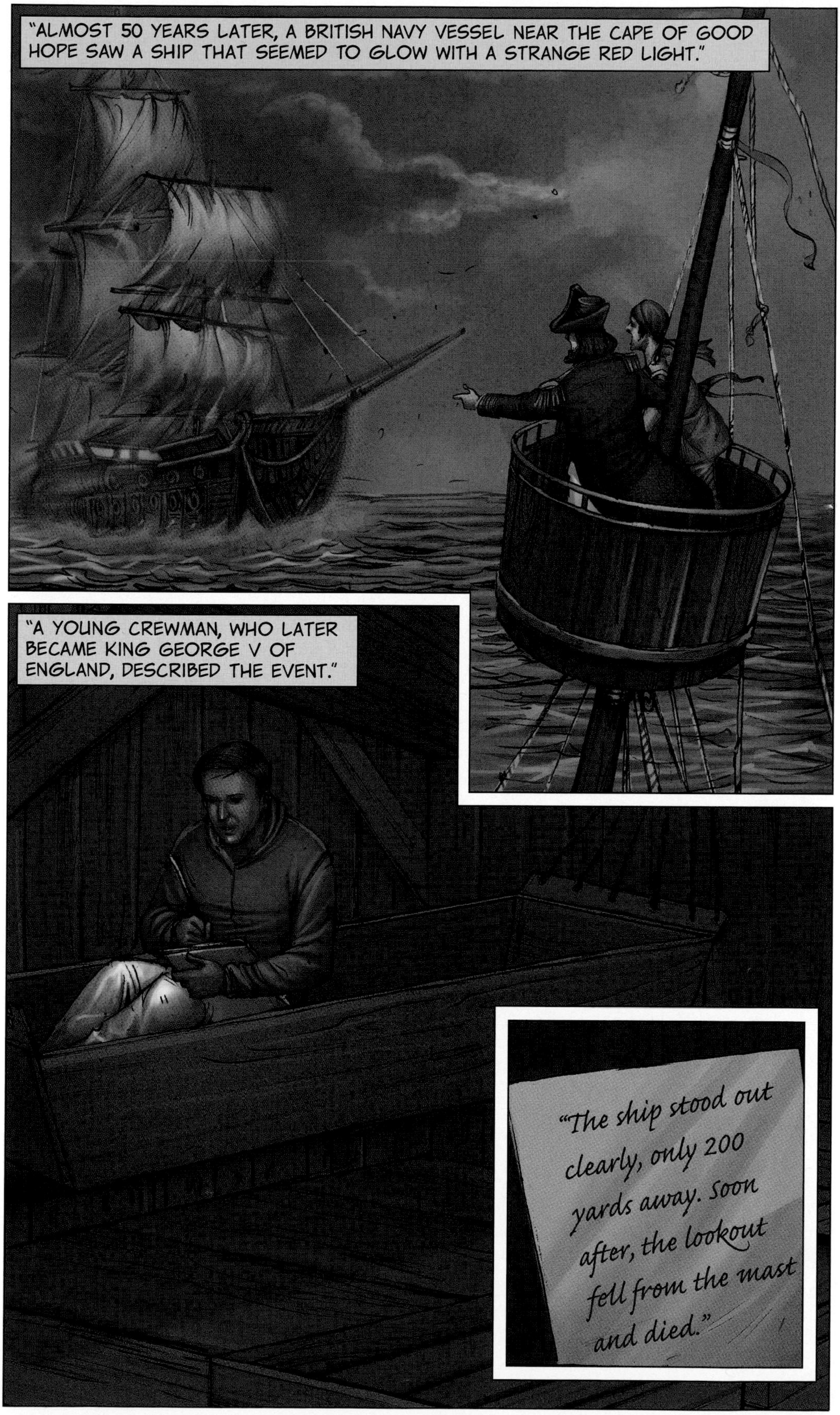
"ALMOST 50 YEARS LATER, A BRITISH NAVY VESSEL NEAR THE CAPE OF GOOD HOPE SAW A SHIP THAT SEEMED TO GLOW WITH A STRANGE RED LIGHT."
"A YOUNG CREWMAN, WHO LATER BECAME KING GEORGE V OF ENGLAND, DESCRIBED THE EVENT."
"The ship stood out clearly, only 200 yards away. Soon after, the lookout fell from the mast and died."

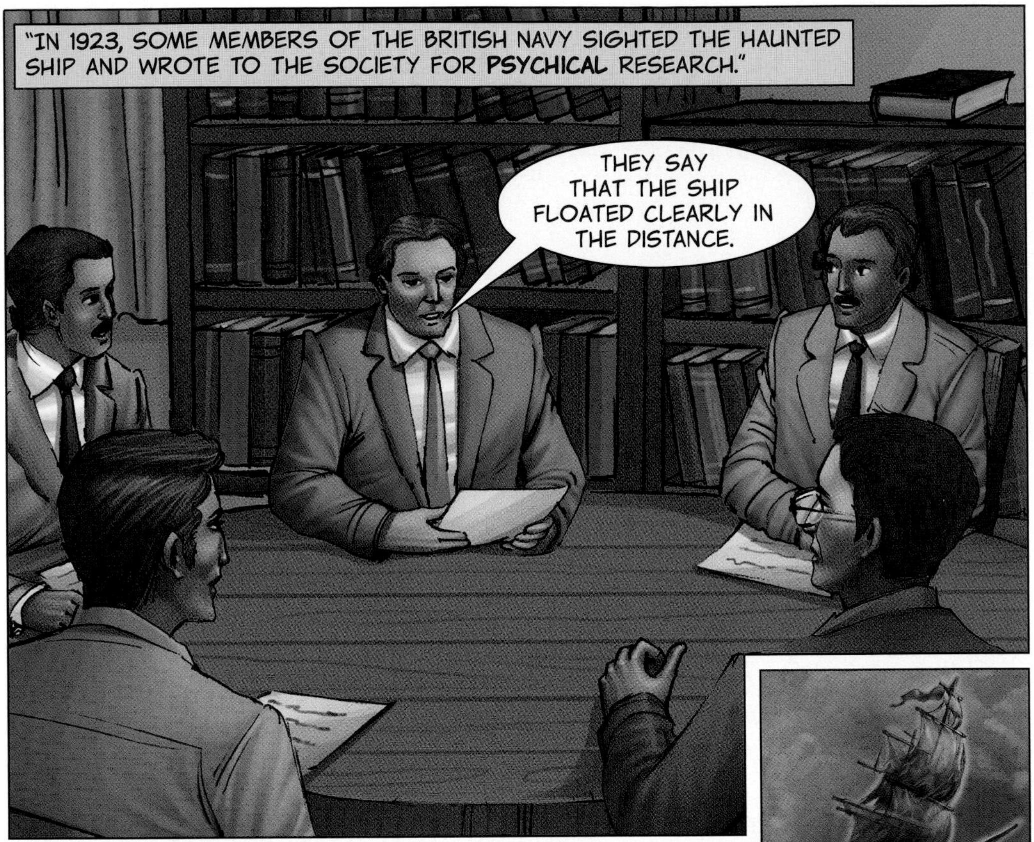
"IN 1923, SOME MEMBERS OF THE BRITISH NAVY SIGHTED THE HAUNTED SHIP AND WROTE TO THE SOCIETY FOR **PSYCHICAL** RESEARCH."
THEY SAY THAT THE SHIP FLOATED CLEARLY IN THE DISTANCE.

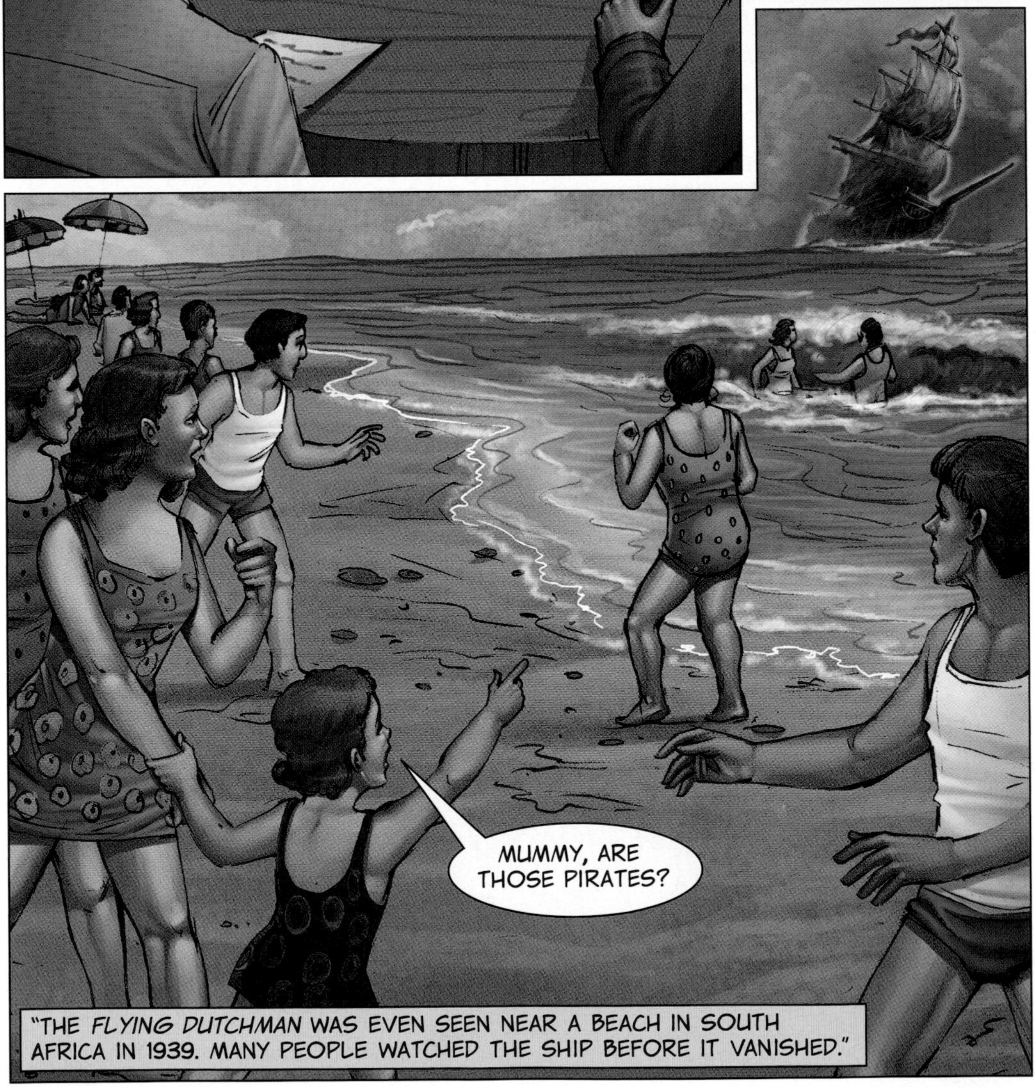
MUMMY, ARE THOSE PIRATES?
"THE *FLYING DUTCHMAN* WAS EVEN SEEN NEAR A BEACH IN SOUTH AFRICA IN 1939. MANY PEOPLE WATCHED THE SHIP BEFORE IT VANISHED."

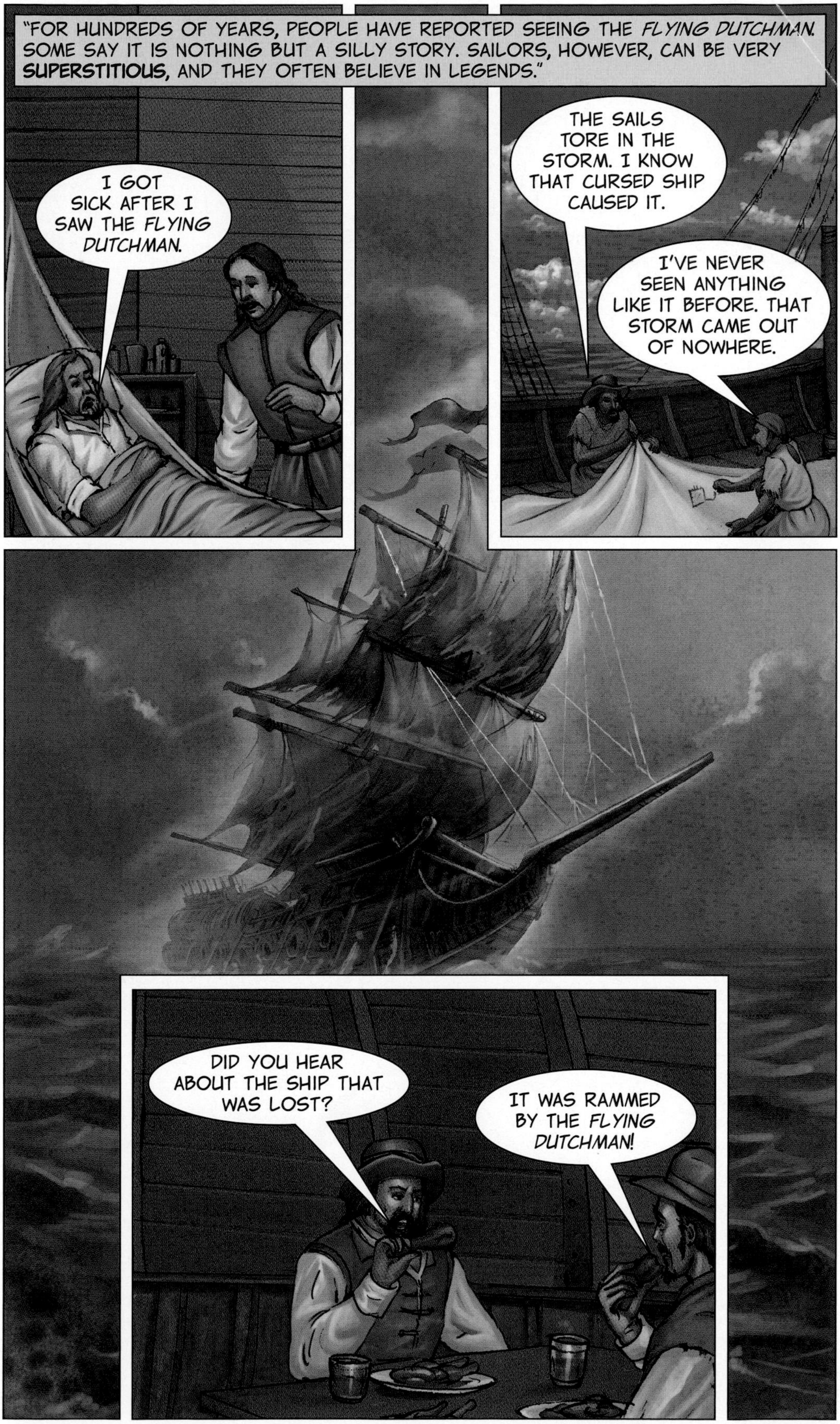
"FOR HUNDREDS OF YEARS, PEOPLE HAVE REPORTED SEEING THE *FLYING DUTCHMAN.* SOME SAY IT IS NOTHING BUT A SILLY STORY. SAILORS, HOWEVER, CAN BE VERY **SUPERSTITIOUS,** AND THEY OFTEN BELIEVE IN LEGENDS."
I GOT SICK AFTER I SAW THE *FLYING DUTCHMAN.*
THE SAILS TORE IN THE STORM. I KNOW THAT CURSED SHIP CAUSED IT.
I'VE NEVER SEEN ANYTHING LIKE IT BEFORE. THAT STORM CAME OUT OF NOWHERE.
DID YOU HEAR ABOUT THE SHIP THAT WAS LOST?
IT WAS RAMMED BY THE *FLYING DUTCHMAN!*

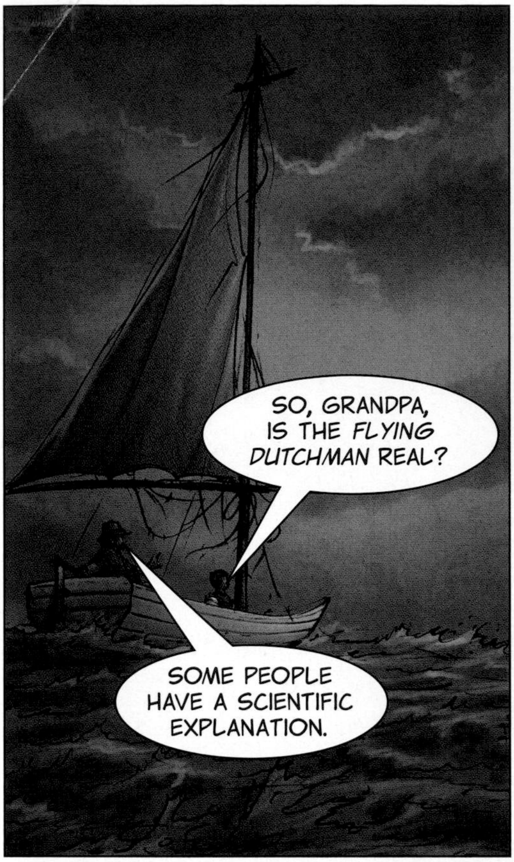
SO, GRANDPA, IS THE *FLYING DUTCHMAN* REAL?
SOME PEOPLE HAVE A SCIENTIFIC EXPLANATION.

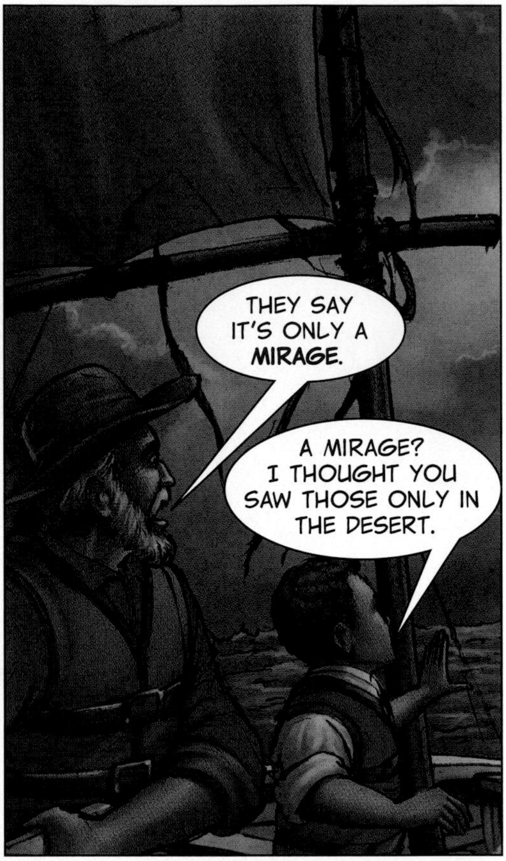
THEY SAY IT'S ONLY A **MIRAGE**.
A MIRAGE? I THOUGHT YOU SAW THOSE ONLY IN THE DESERT.

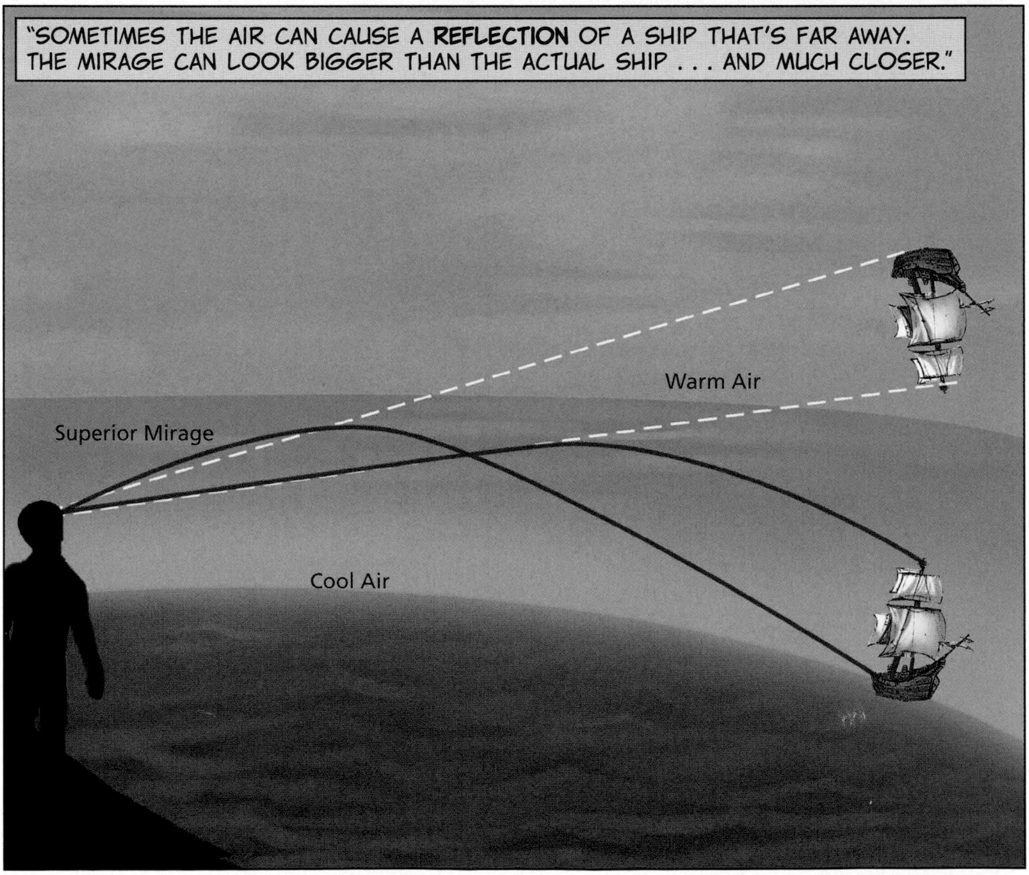
"SOMETIMES THE AIR CAN CAUSE A **REFLECTION** OF A SHIP THAT'S FAR AWAY. THE MIRAGE CAN LOOK BIGGER THAN THE ACTUAL SHIP . . . AND MUCH CLOSER."
Warm Air
Superior Mirage
Cool Air

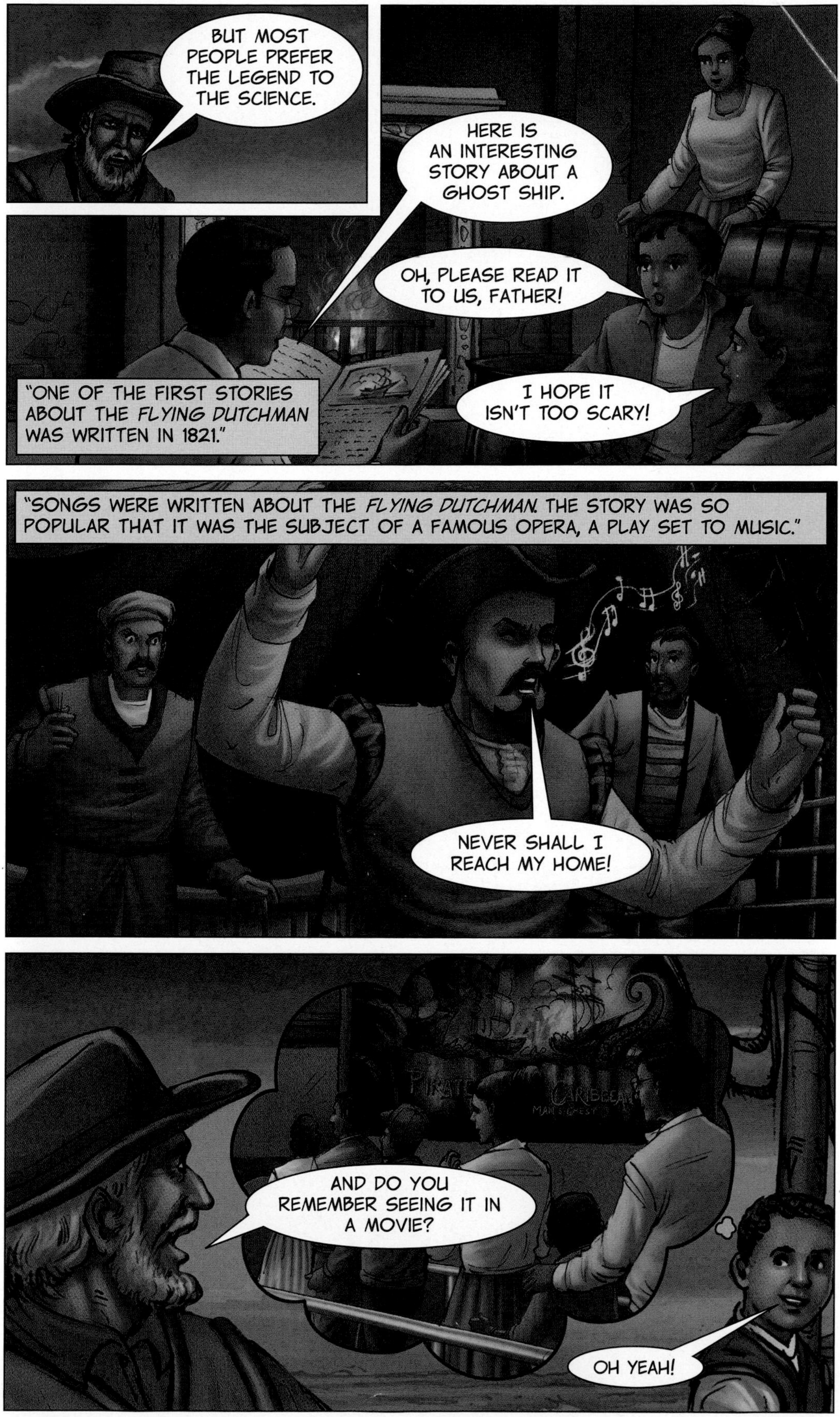

BUT MOST PEOPLE PREFER THE LEGEND TO THE SCIENCE.
HERE IS AN INTERESTING STORY ABOUT A GHOST SHIP.
OH, PLEASE READ IT TO US, FATHER!
"ONE OF THE FIRST STORIES ABOUT THE *FLYING DUTCHMAN* WAS WRITTEN IN 1821."
I HOPE IT ISN'T TOO SCARY!
"SONGS WERE WRITTEN ABOUT THE *FLYING DUTCHMAN*. THE STORY WAS SO POPULAR THAT IT WAS THE SUBJECT OF A FAMOUS OPERA, A PLAY SET TO MUSIC."
NEVER SHALL I REACH MY HOME!
AND DO YOU REMEMBER SEEING IT IN A MOVIE?
OH YEAH!

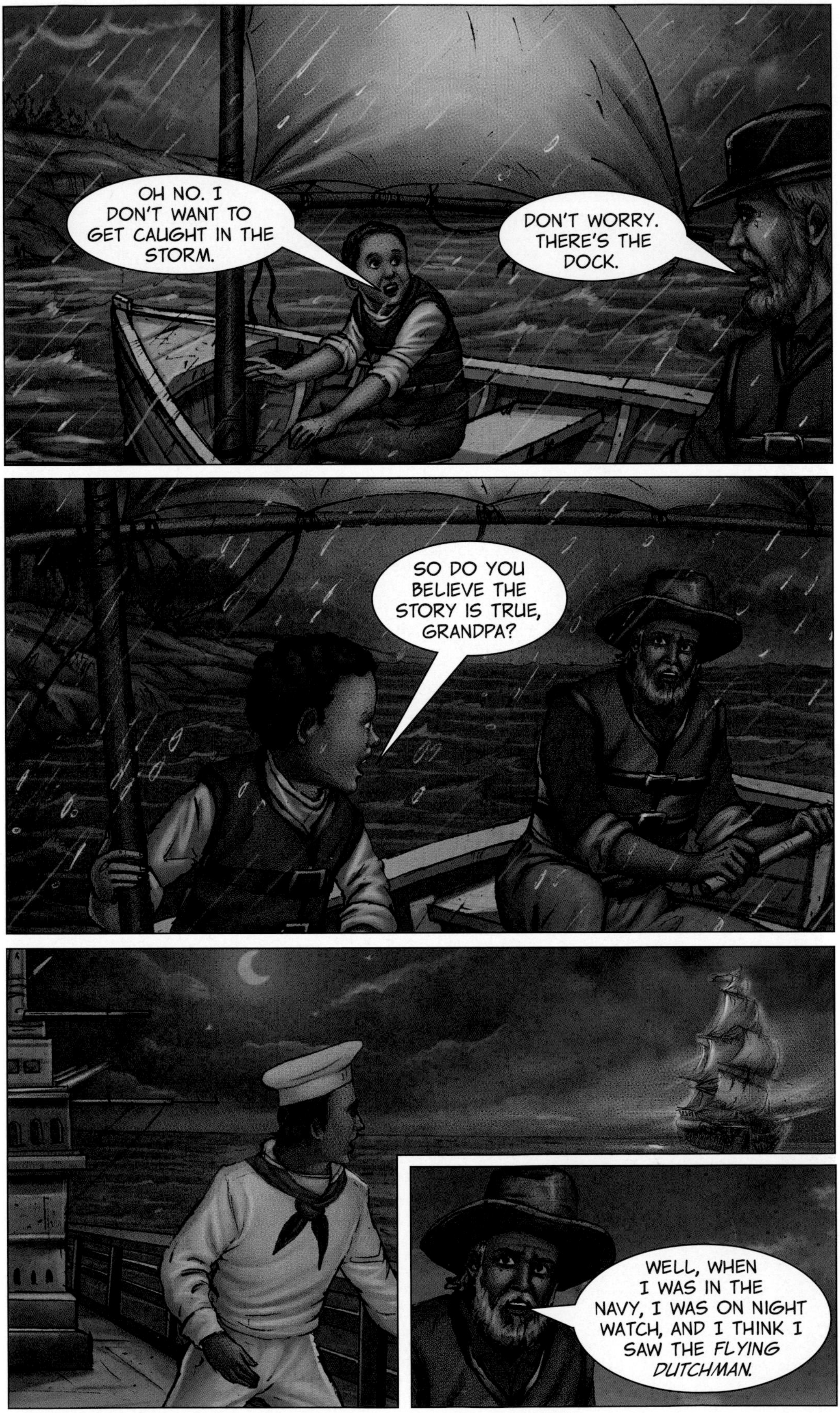
OH NO. I DON'T WANT TO GET CAUGHT IN THE STORM.
DON'T WORRY. THERE'S THE DOCK.
SO DO YOU BELIEVE THE STORY IS TRUE, GRANDPA?
WELL, WHEN I WAS IN THE NAVY, I WAS ON NIGHT WATCH, AND I THINK I SAW THE *FLYING DUTCHMAN.*

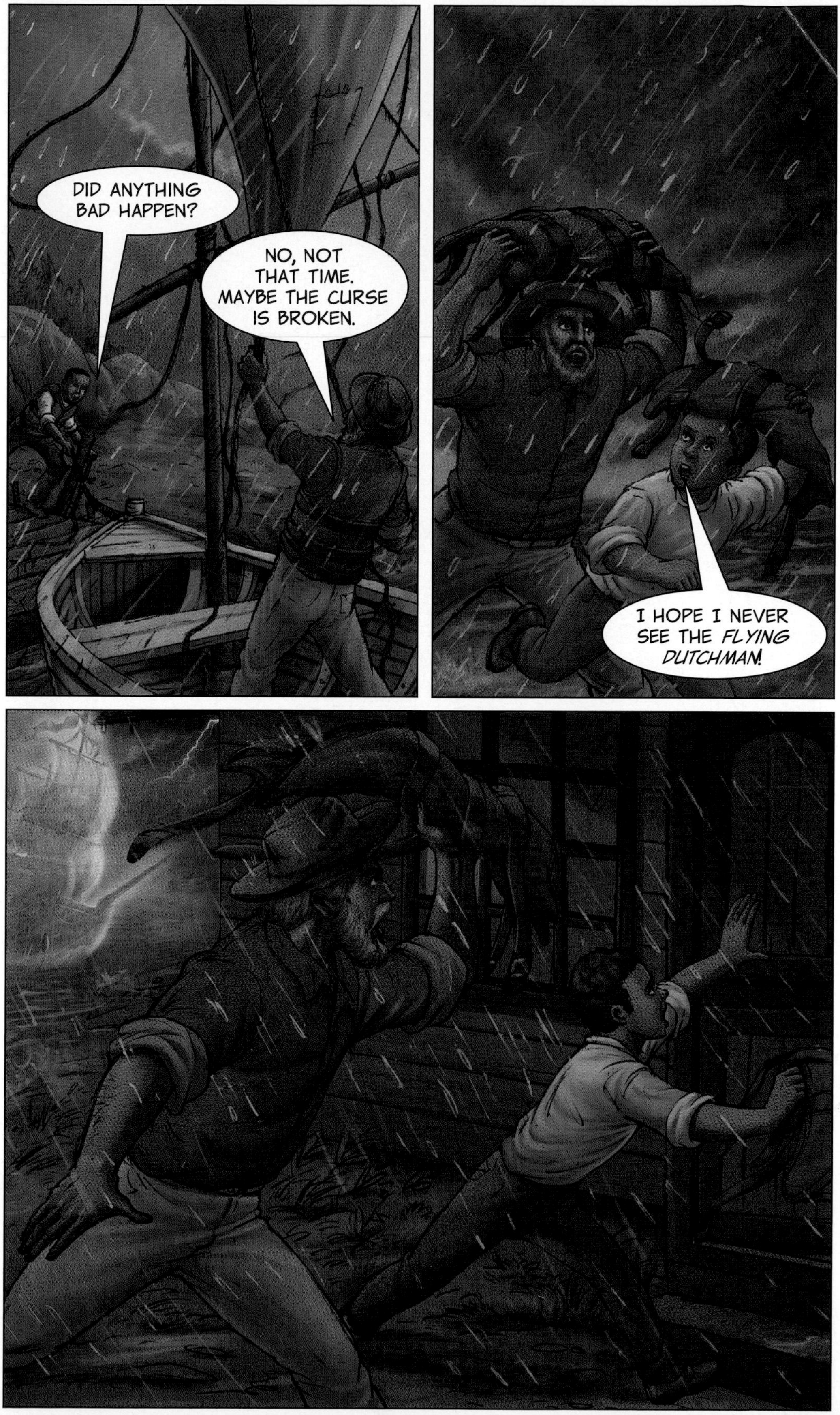
DID ANYTHING BAD HAPPEN?
NO, NOT THAT TIME. MAYBE THE CURSE IS BROKEN.
I HOPE I NEVER SEE THE *FLYING DUTCHMAN*!

# More Ghost Stories

- **"The Rime of the Ancient Mariner"**
  A poem by Samuel Taylor Coleridge. It tells the story of a sailor who brings a curse down on his ship after he shoots a large bird called an albatross. As punishment, the sailor is forced to wander the earth forever to tell his tale.

- **Captain von Falkenberg**
  His story is similar to that of Captain Vanderdecken of the *Flying Dutchman*. In this German version of the story, the captain gambled with the devil and lost. He and his ship were cursed to wander the North Sea forever.

- **The Mysteries of the *Mary Celeste* and the *Carroll A. Deering***
  In 1872, the ship *Mary Celeste* was found drifting in the Atlantic Ocean. In 1921, the ship *Carroll A. Deering* was found grounded off the coast of North Carolina. In both cases, the crews left suddenly and were never found again. No one has ever solved either mystery.

- **The story of the *Caleuche***
  One of the most important legends of Chile, it tells of a ghost ship sailing around Chiloé, a small island off the coast of Chile, at night. The crew is made up of men who have drowned.

- The **Bermuda Triangle**, also known as the **Devil's Triangle**, is an area in the Atlantic Ocean east of Florida and northeast of the Bahamas. Since the 1950s, people have claimed that aircraft and ships have mysteriously disappeared there. Some people have claimed that aliens from outer space may be responsible.

# Glossary

**ahoy** (uh-HOY) Said to greet or call attention to another ship on the water.

**collide** (kuh-LYD) To crash together.

**defied** (dih-FYD) Stood up to authority.

**doomed** (DOOMD) Fated to be a certain way.

**doomsday** (DOOMZ-day) A day of final judgment when the world ends.

**first mate** (FURST MAYT) An officer on a ship ranking just below the captain.

**goods** (GUDZ) Things that people can buy and sell.

**haste** (HAYST) Speed or quickness.

**merchandise** (MER-chun-dys) Goods that are bought and sold.

**mirage** (muh-RAHZH) An effect caused by rays of light and heat that can be seen at sea, in the desert, or on hot pavement. A pool of water appears, or a mirrorlike effect is created in which distant objects can be seen.

**port** (PORT) A town or city with a harbor that ships come in and out of.

**psychical** (SY-kih-kul) Outside the sphere of science or knowledge based on natural laws.

**reflection** (rih-FLEK-shun) The image of something seen on a shiny surface.

**route** (ROOT) The path a person takes to get somewhere.

**superstitious** (soo-per-STIH-shus) Believing in something that cannot be logically explained.

**treacherous** (TREH-chuh-rus) Full of danger.

**trim** (TRIM) To adjust the sails to get the right position.

**vow** (VOW) A sacred promise.

# Index

# Websites

Due to the changing nature of Internet links, PowerKids Press has developed an online list of websites related to the subject of this book. This site is updated regularly. Please use this link to access the list:

www.powerkidslinks.com/jggs/dutch/